Flee

Flee

Calvin Walds

Flee © 2021, Calvin Walds. All rights reserved. No part of this book may be used or reproduced without consent from the author or publisher except in the case of brief quotations appropriated for use in articles and reviews.

Published by Split/Lip Press
6710 S. 87th St.
Ralston, NE 68127
www.splitlippress.com

ISBN: 978-1-952897-11-5

Cover Design by David Wojciechowski

Editing by Lauren Westerfield

Dear Reader:

I'm interested in the idea of there being an 'outside' to all of this. Getting outside as in escaping, as in being outside of systems or structures or institutions or physical spaces of power (the capacity to control behavior or the management of human bodies in the form of racialized biopower), getting outside of confinement, detention, and imprisonment.

What constitutes the outside?

In the context of my own work and my own body, it is an escape from systems that positions people of color close to peripheries, to margins, to being watched, caught, and captured, to confinement . . . in short: to death. 'Outside' and escaping may be easier to conceptualize when one thinks of actual physical structures—the plantation, the slave ship, the prison, the public housing building, the street, the nation-state, the border, the detention center, the handcuffs, the bars of steel. But there is, or must be, or could be, something metaphysical about escape.

I am both looking for what is outside of this and recognizing that when one makes it 'outside' one is very likely to still be 'in it', as Fred Moten said.

Contents

Detroit	12
Aaliyah	19
Paris	24
On the American Colony	35
In the Summer, after the bombing	44
Watching: Hargeisa and Ramallah	51
Drone Lexicon	56
Bourgeois memory prolapse	64
California	69
River Bed	75

DETROIT

Growing up we held drum circles in the living room. The life box pulsed. The room was large, filled with plants and art – pothos, swiss cheese monstera leaves, viper's bowstring, my father's and grandfather's oil work of Orishas, sculptures from the African World Festival held downtown. No couches or tables, just chairs assembled from throughout the house, and us together, the conscious blacks of Detroit.

The vibrational politics of diaspora. An affective regime of red, black, and green. Imagine the Black Panthers just carrying tuning forks. Striking them at the precinct.

I would sneak outside. I wasn't embarrassed when I heard the measured madness down the block of adjacent sub-urban homes.

I like circulations. They feel dangerous. I used to backstroke down and up the lanes of my high school swimming pool. Water opened my eyes. I've felt most full of life while tipsy at the beach. The contradictions weren't apparent or consuming yet.

Summers in Detroit were not for cracking open the fire hydrant but taking day trips to a blue white lake. Shallow enough and full of plants and rocks. Only tired adult eyes on a childhood memory of a beach with a grass shore could connect our arrival to their gradual departure. Like the lake, they too eventually become all black. The reaction to all the talk of death in theory will be a relishing of life.

Levinas speaks of the *originality of escape*. He says *it is a matter of getting out of being by a new path*.[1] When I eat at chain restaurants while home, usually one of my old classmates works there.

---

1 Levinas *On Escape* (1935)

This isn't about poesies. Every song I listen to seems to be about longing. *Choose your worth and say it's not there.*[2] Longing is my political apparatus. I still dance in the mirror. And people still wonder why we won't just accept the world.

I'm reading Adorno about the tension between the conditional and the unconditional. He says, "The unconditional becomes fact, the conditional an immediate essence."[3]

Conditions, in my American mind, becomes *contract*, ligaments obliged.

I'm in my bedroom looking for that which is bereft of context, roughness, privy, or scorn. I can't find a single thing.

---

[2] Blood Orange- "I Know" (Freetown Sound, 2016)

[3] Theodore Adorno, *The Stars Down to Earth, and other essays on the Irrational in Culture* (1994)

I text a friend about a photograph of James Baldwin. I write: *it seems to be about everything: apprehension, sadness, pride, fear. An unconditional and atemporal apposition.* They say: *I think it's his eyes.*

Fugitivity is a sacrifice, a spiraling that expels outward. The dissolution into parts. A fugue of melodies, voices, inhabiting the same bracketed space, falling and twisting at the hip, into and onto each other.

I want to be so close that I can smell it. We left Bossa Nova, a club in Bushwick, together. The night was about making techno Black again. We stopped and I admitted under a construction scaffold that I want to feel desperate for something.

Who doesn't? Can you imagine being forlorn or tossed or whiplashed? I imagine these are conceptual experiences. I'm tired of the neutrality of neon saturation and consumption; of being just ok.

---

4 "eye shot" 2020

Flee

In a fugue one melody is the subject, the other a counter, vying for the subject position. A replacement: fungible. Then there is dissociative fugue, a total or partial elision of memory. An otherwise oblivion.

Some call this natal alienation. This is a reference to Orlando Patterson.

My mother was pregnant with my sister the year her brother Kurt, my uncle, was killed. *I go up and down, up and down*, a singer from Atlanta named Abra reminds us. Polarity. Why all the talk of lives?

I'm afraid the wi-fi is being throttled and I just locked the patio door.

Can I tell you something? This is a continuation. A tangle of sunlit priors? My uncle's murder happened on Valentine's Day in 1992. Princess Nokia, a Bronx rapper named after the cellphone company, has an album titled 1992.

I say: *Cupid's arrow has always been a violent metaphor.*

You say: *that makes me think of violets.*

I like clothes from the 1990s: Starter Brand, Jerzees, NBA apparel. Maybe these are what my uncle might have worn or admired. Officers Theodore Briseno and Timothy Wind were acquitted in the beating of Rodney King in April, a month before my sister was born. I was shot five minutes into paintballing with high school students.

At house parties, I end up on the couch. What did we talk about? Make sure you don't tell anyone at all.

I finish a cup of water as I look at an image of planks of wood painted with black oil bundled together with sealant. The sculpture is titled 'A Memorial for Uncle Tom'.[5]

---

5 Postscript: I checked the internet. This sculpture doesn't exist.

James Baldwin and Uncle Tom are both dead. Jack Whitten's *Black Monolith* is a tribute to Baldwin.

From my window in Detroit, I get used to a certain aesthetical politics: things distressed and repurposed, an exposure of pipes, bricks, wood beams, broken concrete, flickering light.

On the day that I wrote this Jack Whitten had been dead for six days. Baldwin died in 1987. I wish someone would upload the video of both of their funerals. I would stream them simultaneously, waiting for a solace to find me.

AALIYAH

In the video for '4 Page Letter' Aaliyah walks through a forest in leather, stumbles upon Maroons.

There are rings of fire, motorcycles, and caged dancers in the forest together. Her choreography feels simple but evades imitation. Aaliyah was raised in Detroit.

There are symphonies and operas about the lives of Malcolm X and W.E.B Dubois but not Aaliyah. I cried at an operatic performance where a man hated his body. We sat in soft chairs and watched as he writhed and flailed on stage in white underwear. In my room, I imagine thrusting my hips like Aaliyah's side dancers.

I learned of Aaliyah's death on a playground at recess in sixth grade. Some girls made posters with cut out magazine pictures. On the radio, they played her songs on repeat.

One day I want to write a 'take-down' piece. Get paranoid and write about a 'war' on a value or institution. I want to be described as unpredictable. I want to see someone snap.

Franco Bifo observes the hyper-stimulated body as one that is simultaneously alone and hyper-connected. The collective unconscious of twenty-somethings can relate.

In Harlem we brought the wooden dining table painted blue out onto the roof for my roommate's event, a party full of former liberal art school students. I woke up the next morning on top of the table. Franco Bifo Berardi writes of the danger of foreclosing the imagination, a liquidating sale of the soul. We should not feel comfort in easy predictions.

>

Did you finish reading the book about history? "I did. It's almost as if it had no bearing."

I ask how you got me into Show Me The Body in Ridgewood. You show how you whispered to the doorman, "It's just one more person." He seemed surprised and relieved at the calamity of it all.

To look at the sky—and I do—both the sun and the moon are both visible. Holding the totality of the absence or presence of light.

I want to not have to care about land or soil or rock or bush to just realize how flat and bright everything is—even the hills—and you ask, "can a fragment feel free?"

>

I ran from my group of friends after leaving a club. We were walking uptown and there was talk of getting food. I slipped around a corner and kept going.

6 Manhattan (2019)

The "I" writing to "you" lacks self-sufficiency. The lyrical cannot stand alone. I am reading Levinas again. Did you know Levinas wrote about escape?

Did you know that one can feel both shame and relief after a happening?

Yes.

Text messages are landing softly onto my devices. Levinas is telling me that the "I" needs "you."

For a moment, in the early 2010s, rap wanted to sound big. There was Kanye and Jay Z's H*A*M, Rick Ross's B.M.F (Blowing Money Fast), and Lil Wayne's *John* with a *chopper in the car*.

In the summer of 2012, the year after *John* was released, I was living in Paris, where roses were obsolete.

PARIS

To announce an ending. Obsoleting is key to liberalism, capitalism, and the array of industrial objects surrounding you in your apartment or house. With each arrival of "new" is the ending of the prior—a racialized democracy of neoliberal excess.

A rose is obsolete, perhaps, because as Stein predicted: a rose is a rose is a rose is a chain of exports on Amazon conveyor belts. But I'm not caught in the cult of originals. I'll gladly take a print of a Basquiat painting.

Deleuze finds potential in the act of reproduction for error or repudiation of the institutionalized prototype. The copy could become something else. Spring is not simply a period of rebirth—it is a season of glitch.

Four proposals on obsolution and the "new poesis":

1. To render an object obsolete is to proclaim that said object is not only not passe or kitsch, but is wholly incompatible with the pulsing, dispossessing, and precarious futurity automatically rolling in . . .

2. The obsolete object may need to be buried in a landfill of cultural-technological waste filled with sentimental respectfully representational images that can no longer respond to a fracturing and suturing world in which the bar is the boiling ocean.

3. The rose is not only no longer useful; it is not as swift as new roses, not as shiny as the images of "new poesis", nor arrives with as much clout or grant funding.

4. The rose, and perhaps the image of the bough, the sappy guise, is therefore defunct. But one should not despair, as while Williams Carlos Williams may write "love is at an end" he clarifies that "it is at the edge of the petal that love waits."

In Paris, I walk out the Metro wearing big over-ear headphones with the music still playing. The sound leaks. A woman shushes me in a restaurant. I am broke and order appetizers as meals, share plates with others.

Appropriation and extraction are about proliferation and spreading the 'feel' of something, the 'sound' of it, the main parts. You get the experience without the real deal, the rose "cuts with cutting," a house of pure empty aesthetic horror from which you leave unscathed, transformed, and ready to begin your day.

>

I have standards. Ok? I'm not going around wearing just any old Desert Storm T-shirt I find at the thrift store like I'm some middle school kid who can't tell the difference between a pair of Converse and a Ballistic Missile. I'm not trying to flatten everything out like some AI parceling out your Aunt's birthday resolutions right before some dark posts from Russia telling you not to vote because Clinton got reincarnated twice. I'm not saying we should just drop a drone on them like a couple of bumblebees in a field of lavender. I have standards. Ok?

Rick Ross assures us that celebrity does not foreclose the necessity or possibility of violence. Rick Ross channels Frantz Fanon that way. In Paris, there was always wine.

Like a good radical, I'm trying to strike a colonial counterbalance by evoking Fanon in the memory haze of Paris. I was told to love France before I was told of an otherwise history of occupation and hubris.

In the outskirts of Paris, we visit a Roma camp. Discriminatory French law and culture compels their constant movement.

A friend dares me to blackout from the meager food and generous alcohol platter they set out for us. The Roma are all short with weathered skin. I spill enough alcohol that it seems I am doing it intentionally, pouring one out for the ancestors.

It is perhaps the anxieties of seeing a state and citizenry's violence stare back at you. Violence from another state, *Brother from Another Planet*. The Roma spoke of an existence carved out against local decrees against them. *Who can relate?*

In Paris, I never visit James Baldwin's former home.

I instead stay out into the night in Paris with S, a free spirit from Turkey. Meeting over gin, I ask if there is anyone in our fellowship group they fancy. They smile and say yes.

I am supposed to be living with a single older woman in St. Denis, but I rarely make the trek out to the suburbs. Instead, I sleep on floors or split one side of the beds of others. For a few nights, the older woman worries, but quickly starts to go to bed before my return.

I have cousins that are incarcerated for life. Incarcerated is sonically and ontologically close to incinerated. I remember standing outside the jail in downtown Detroit next to my mother. She raised her fist in a Black power salute. I hope someone in the jail could see her.

To break a sound or flow is about opening space. Emergence is mercurial, a reflection of a world in which there have been few true cessations and more of a series of rearrangements, patterns rearticulated and diverged.

>

If breaking departures have the potential to be radical as a measure of distance, how far does an emergent break have to leave *to leave?*

>

---

7 Brooklyn (2020)

The moon glowing honeysuckle. I felt it in my hands like I was washing dishes and the water turned hot.

We're walking selflessly and I just want to get back and get into my bed.

>

There's a thin blue line crackling there in the middle of the road and my boy looks at me and says, "We've got to cross it."

I'm interested in words whose meaning has been evacuated, words whose users have abandoned the symbolic function of language.

By this, I mean the way that Future the rapper dissolves the word "Wicked" or "Coupe" in his repetition leaving some *thing* out of the sentence: a subject, an action, a cause, a ground, or condition.

In undergrad we would stage actions like class walk outs and disruptions of professors. A professor once pleaded with me in a hallway because she felt that she was losing control over the class. Aren't actions about redistributing power?

I also did solo actions: I barricaded myself in a dorm room by locking the door.

8 Ratnagiri, India (2019)

S corners me in the apartment of Nick from Cologne. *I can tell that you love me.* That I loved them was because they had read.

The consensus is that the sound of rap changed because rappers stopped selling and started using drugs. Love was easier then.

That night of the cornering we all danced in a living room. Epic rap is about power, *fully loaded clips*. S and I ended up in the hallway against the wall. Someone stumbled on us: *You two should come back.*

The night I am writing this I am watching a slow film in an ambient daze. Long shots of shipping containers floating atop ships that make whales seem as small as silver fish.

The containers are primary colors and appear agentic and lazy. The film is vaguely political, in a way most things are.

The containers remind me of a freeway next to a valley in Detroit full of old train cars. Sometimes four are stacked on top of each other.

The containers sit there rusting of a time when Detroit was economically active, a stuttered lapse touched by snow and shine.

There is a restaurant downtown where you can eat inside a container with limited seating.

The film cuts and sutures the images of ships and the smoke flumes of ambiguous factories to gesture toward industrialized global trade.

The suture is the film's innovation as the shipping containers give way to images of automated workers hammering in a way that suggests that one is the other or the same.

I had a dream last night that a painter and I released everyone from a prison. There was no explanation as to why, beyond that they needed to be free. There was no pretense about safety. The releasing was banal, quiet and unlike the popular depiction of prison breaks as mutant brutes steaming back into the population cracking their knuckles and beating their fists into palms.

Afterwards we all went swimming.

In Paris we talk often of the Burka Ban. To my American mind, such prejudice does not feel surprising. Friends and strangers enjoy telling me that couscous is France's most popular food, but I already know that most colonizers enjoy eating the food of the people they colonized.

Is French Empire a term? French troops are still in Mali.

I know why we say Niger (Nigre) the way that we do. Côte d'Ivoire. République du Sénégal. Renoi. Fanon's *Lived Experience Of The Black*. I'm apprehensive about watching Ousmane Sembane's *Black Girl* and I know I'm missing out.

9

---

9 Contrast (2020)

On the American Colony

I won't lie: I've imagined the experience of having a classier colonizer. American colonies only get the benefits of Denny's, diabetes, and a heavy fidelity to a place that doesn't exist.

I'm thinking of my foremothers as I type "the shipped held in the slave vessel's belly." Google wants me to change "shipped" to "shipment." So that you would read: "The shipment was held in the slave vessel's belly".

This might be what Joy James might call the "captive maternal".

In an email chain, we are asked to introduce ourselves. One person writes back "*I am a Black American (descendant of slaves)*." I wondered who the parenthetical reminder was for.

We declare "mission accomplished" before asking "are you ok after the bombing?" Our failure to await an answer is due in part to our unsavory relationship to the passage of time.

It is not only the chokehold, not only the fallen body in which no one but the world noticed. The actuality of the violence against us shorn as it is from proper symbolism can best be described as "demoded" with a precedent that is not an event but a totality, so omnipresent as to be the generalized field.

Geometric is such a breakage. William Carlos Williams once described this as: "standing and fallen patches of standing water."

S and I aren't shy. We kiss in the backseat of a cab. During a lunch break from a day of civil society speakers speaking to us civil society leaders of the future. We go back to Saint-Denis to make use of an empty apartment. Saint-Denis is a formerly industrial suburb currently changing its economic base.

hiding there in caveats

a suckle of orange

layers of capriciousness, a bed

a cover of river, swiping the moon

piles of trees unrooted, unhinged, crumples of wire and old

plumbing pipes lying hiding, gripping a dozen

brooms, feet shorn in seashells,

old leather whips, old living room rugs, smashed shards of flutes, crinkled sweaters,

red tulips, lawn mulch, insect spray, wood laminate cabinetry, counterfeit shoes,

mouth guards, goggles, doughnut boxes, middle school textbooks, metal detectors, gold watches, broken chicken eggs, printer ink, beach sand, a concentrate of tropical fruits, covering my legs and thighs in

sticky catechism

10 Hargeisa, Somaliland (2016)

I am watching Musa Okwonga's performance of 'The Migrant Manifesto'. The video begins with a close-up on Okwonga's lower face. Okwonga's reserved speech is forceful but never thrusting.

He begins:

> We have been called many names.
>
> Illegals. Aliens. Guest Workers. Border crossers. Undesirables. Exiles. Criminals. Non-citizens. Terrorists. Thieves. Foreigners. Invaders. Undocumented.

There is a pause before calling upon the names as he channels others who have spoken and wrote about the evacuation of self, being, and humanness, of the false names that have been layered upon those made expendable.

I say, get on the ground right now so we can be planted like a seed of Neptune. Grow into sassafras used as shade by the lakeside with a pier and the plastic paddle boats you can rent for twenty dollars.

Musa calls upon the humans those names represent, the humans who remain vulnerable because of those names, the humans who are more than those names.

His uttering of the names does not blame or identify the culprit.

At the San Francisco Museum of Modern Art there is a room with three large screens. John Akomfrah, a member of the Black Audio Film Collective projects images that suggest beauty and violence. On one screen a sun set, another a poached whale is sliced open in a massive spilling.

Children in the screening room sprawl on the floor until their parents shudder awake and direct them out.

In representations of post-industrial cities like Detroit, the crumbling spatial is shown to exist outside the assimilated (acquisitive, white, liberal). This outsider status is claimed as the cause of the social and political decay that impact the people living in bounded space.

Such thinking forgoes any analysis of neoliberal and racist practices and people that abandoned post-industrial urban cities. Under such thinking the processes of assimilation and gentrification becomes a moral obligation and inevitability. Success is integrating a land of Black conditions into Landed Property: soft liberal capital capitalism, fast-casual restaurants, direct-to-consumer chain stores.

I stay in the screening room, standing close to several others standing in front and behind and beside me watching the fisherman's routine processing of the whale's body. The film is not dated. Neither the quality nor the hairstyles of the fishermen give a hint as to what decade the hunt had occurred. As anachronistic and timeless as the flickering shots of butterflies and cresting waves. As if to say we are not and weren't ever this body.

As if to say, it is an impossibility to go and stay outside.

As when Frank Ocean says he'd rather live outside on *Siegfried*.

Me: Outside of what, or who, or when?

Frank: Outside madness or grief somehow, outside political time.

Me: A winter storm is a quite literal swirling of whiteness, cold and indifferent.

Frank: Outside could be a want to exist as otherwise, as not-already.

I used to get haircuts once a week. These reaching lips. Nose spread in the center of my face. My nose was inherited. To exist means that I am connected to something somewhere at every point in time.

I bought canvases and oil paints and they lay on the floor behind a potted plant.

On the Shlomo mix of the posthumous Aaliyah cut 'Enough Said' he slows the track down to the point that Aaliyah's voice morphs into a deep, slurred nostalgia. *Can you talk to me? Tell me what you need?* I'm not sure I've ever pleaded to a lover or to a State. Can you imagine doing either?

The purple beauty of mourning is bound up in crawling to the reader, to the state, to the someone who might call me *boy*. I find *boy* and *man* overdetermined. I want to write a poem that calls the reader *baby*. I want to ask the reader to cry with *me* lest you die.

How to live in a world designed in the image of my flaying? Cinematic representations of simultaneity bound up in births. A time-lapse montage of flowers blooming, clouds stuttering, long pan-shots of grassy windswept fields, a new-born baby with rose-flamed cheeks crying at the first touch of room temperature. All are yoked in a single collapsed frame, as to say life and death are sequential and symbolic and interval. Can you talk to me?

A chopped slowing down evokes the significance of language, of the ask, of the impossibility of an answer ever being sufficient enough for what is requested, some kind of metaphysical wanting that English could never provide.

In the summer, after the bombing

In March of 2013, the year after the summer in Paris, two homemade bombs exploded near the finish line of the Boston Marathon.

With member names like Juicy J and Crunchy Black there is a hint toward Three 6 Mafia's concern with the *quality* of the physical. Not just the tongue but the saliva that coats it.

I watched footage of Rodney King being asked to display his physical wounds in a courtroom, and how he repudiated the attempt to say his attack was due to his racialized body.

Perhaps that malignant divergence of harm and cause is the world.

Perhaps, then, what is required are remedies or policies that improve the quality of life for the marginalized in a way that works outside the world we reside in. Sanctioned methods of 'improving' human life compromise the ecosystem and make individuals more vulnerable.

What is good?

>

S is living in DC and working for a member of the United States Congress. In 2013 this is still something to aspire to. I spend part of the summer in Ghana and return to the United States a little sad and a little angry. I am tan, and have started to lock my hair. I end up splitting a studio for a few days that turns into weeks with a friend in DC.

Three 6 Mafia is famous for winning an Academy Award, the first rap group to do so in a year in which there was an insurgence of southern sweaty gleaming beats.

One of the suspects of the Boston Marathon Bombing is found hiding under a boat in a backyard. S is having a small get together in Georgetown.

I decide to go, but with the caveat of bringing a Date.

I tell S that the Date is just a Friend. I do not tell the Friend that S and I had a recent and complicated history. At the party, there is another Friend from Boston.

Day time sleeping sounds like violets in a clear carafe. I took a carafe to the beach to keep water. I imagined hauling a gallon of sea back to the apartment to scrub with. I was the only black boy in that part of the ocean as far as the eye can see. Imagine if sight weren't limited to the horizon—if we could see from coast to coast.

At a bonfire in Brattleboro someone sang: 'this land is your land, this land is my land'.

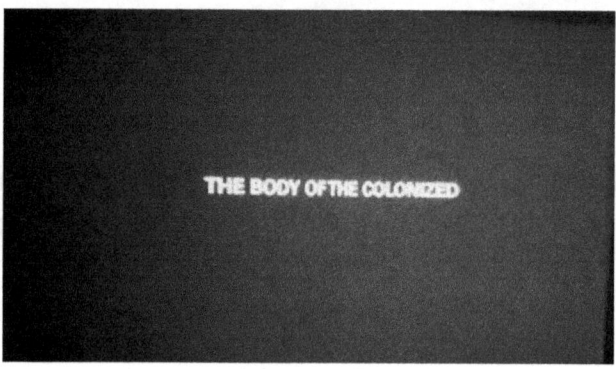

The sacrifice of precarious laborers reminds me of the Flint Water Crisis and the protesting miners shot dead in South Africa and of the uber drivers who keep telling me that they've been up and driving since 4am and of the autoworkers in my home city who worked with their hands and backs in a radical sacrifice of *time* for a commodity.

Three 6 Mafia's song *Who Run It?* sounds like a middle school fight soundtracked by a marching band. It is my favorite and is best described as an American Epic.

I keep pausing *I Don't Want to Sleep Alone* by Tsai Ming Liang to take screenshots which I legally can't reproduce here. Imagine Malaysia 2006: crowded diners with smoking clients, an empty street illuminated by a flickering multicolor light toy, an abandoned construction site filled with sewer water.

The rhyme scheme of Three Six Mafia bars precedes what we now think of as drill rap. The titular question is asked repeatedly with sped up urgency: *Who run it? Who run it? Who run it?*

Possible answers include "I" "You" "We" or "Them".

This closed question is an implicit threat that ensures conflict.

A comment on the YouTube version of the song states: *when this use to come on some body was getting fucked up fo sho.*

At the party I suggest that the bombing is part of a circulation. United States militarism ruining lives and communities abroad. The friend from Boston reminds me, "*Yes, but still . . .* " the *still* exists within what was left unsaid. The Date notices S rubbing my exposed legs. The Date leaves before me.

>

Placelessness is a luxury that this Black American has rarely possessed. A feeling of being imprecisely, of not knowing exactly where and why you are where you are. There is a certain keenness to being in America, a surveilled awareness in the way of my parents' instruction to "always be aware of your surroundings" upon noticing a certain dreaminess to the way I moved through the world. Constantly apprehending or environing the world requires a detachment from presence.

>

An inability to not constantly consider the dilemmas wrought of being, is the seduction of amnesia. My flatmates joined me on the rooftop one morning. All the concrete, the overlapping freeways, the apartments and schools look like detention centers.

11   Costa Rica (2019)

12 San Diego (2018)

Watching: Hargeisa and Ramallah

The last line of *Public Figures* by Jena Osman seems to speak of the centrality of sight within the process of understanding the world: "everything relies on visual confirmation, action no longer sensation."

Osman could be gesturing toward how the generalized reader is like a drone pilot, in that much of our apprehension of the world is through mediated images, and that the physical and the felt is often impossible or inaccessible – that we come to know each other, to feel each other, through sight or virtuality, disembodied projections, holograms, copies, corrupted files, figures and estimations, glitches, mimicries, shadows.

I think about sight often. How we come to see what we think we see. I think about how often what we see is not what is there, or what was there, or what could be there. To see each other beneath and beyond the layers of fabrication and distance that seem to cover the worlds around us in a thick layer.

Osman's project is to take photographs from the line of sight of statues. Soldiers of conquest, imperialism and war, Philadelphia's legacy. She integrates journalistic photographs of soldiers from our contemporary wars in Iraq and other places in the Middle East.

Thread: There is a ticker tape of drone pilot transcripts sourced from YouTube.

All poets are journalists.

Osman reminds us that monuments are some of the most invisible objects within our landscapes. Even more invisible are the violences each statue represents. In the proliferation of decontextualized images of war, are we, too, forgetting the violences that marks and shreds the world?

Images coming out of Gaza of Israeli soldiers shooting live ammunition into the bodies and hearts and limbs of Palestinian protestors equipped with rocks and bottles.

In Palestine we are watching the process of colonization.

I think about this as we drive through a plantation in Mississippi. The violence that created this space, of settler colonialism and enslavement, resides both in history and in the present.

A panel of civic leaders remarked that Mississippians bond over food, just as the enslaved who cooked for and fed and nursed their enslavers did. I ride through the plantation, gazing, *not touching*, thinking of memories, like the Blade Runner *Replicants* Osman mentions, that both belong and are utterly ulterior to me.

Mississippi is beautiful. The blood has been washed with the laundry. Clean white clothes. It created the nothingness that Osman observes her statues watching. The sculptures seem to be looking at nothing in particular; they have a gaze, but they don't have a need for it.

13 Occupied Palestine (2018)

You wonder about your experiment, whether it has any value at all.

What is there to see but some trees, a bird, a nondescript skyscraper?

What is there to see in Gaza but the historical present. Do we all understand what we are looking at? Can we agree that what we see reflects the violence that made the world? Of course not.

"To see the sigh of sighted stone you activate the idea."[14]

---

14 Jena Osman, *Public Figures*

DRONE LEXICON

On March 7th, 2016, a United States led drone and armed aircraft strike killed more than 150 people, many sitting under trees, in Mogadishu. I was 1,500 kilometers away, teaching, breathing, sheltering in Somaliland.

Drone music feels generative, as if one can hear the propelling of a landscape-wide interior fan, the continuation and unfolding of itself in a set of sonic grammars, the tenors, modulations, and bounds provided by the artist.

Deep splash and spreading. In a virtual silver pool with impossibly smooth water, the foreground of that slight dissonant shakiness. Two notes without affinity find each other, a flashing vibration like a satellite pulse. Then the crest, the emanation, this commingling.

I tend toward 'warm' drone music, an appellation that perhaps gestures at the haptic qualities of the genre. Is warm perhaps a stand in for slowness, measured swells, the soft rigidity of a synthetically produced atmosphere of spiraling at strict intervals? The only interruption is the song's ending. Most lasting from fifteen minutes to an hour without feeling repetitious, allowing the listener to rest in the song's tunnel.

There is no landing in silence. You capsize far from the shore, no instant when all the waves are at rest. Like the ocean, there is always another forming, rolling, and rising next to the other. This discernment requires seeing the drone, because there is no referent timbre, no instrument to point to but the generation itself. To listen is to see and to see is to feel the approach of the drone's fire on skin.

Perhaps war is everything, which is to say that everything is war. There and not there. Ended but always on-going. Rippling out across the landscape. That sculptures are always armed. The bird landed at the mouth of the revolver.

Osman includes images of her camera wrapped with Velcro. As if to say, my hands made this sight. My hands made this poem. A ticker tape of the artist at the bottom of each page.

Rodney King is asked to lift his shirt to show his seared skin. The police officers tasered him. I rub my computer screen, my hands impossible.

15 Occupied Palestine (2018)

The pitch of a covert attack. The isolation of a strand of water. Drones are privy to our bodies. Our bodies privy to collapsing warmth, hiding it inside the edges of our mouths. Think of civilian death both within and outside American borders. Sigh into a microphone. Look at the resultant waves. Stretch the file of your sigh into infinitesimal qualities, climb into the valley, greet the inhabitants, learn the history of the sigh, follow its waves, falling and folding, folding and falling.

16　Occupied Palestine (2018)

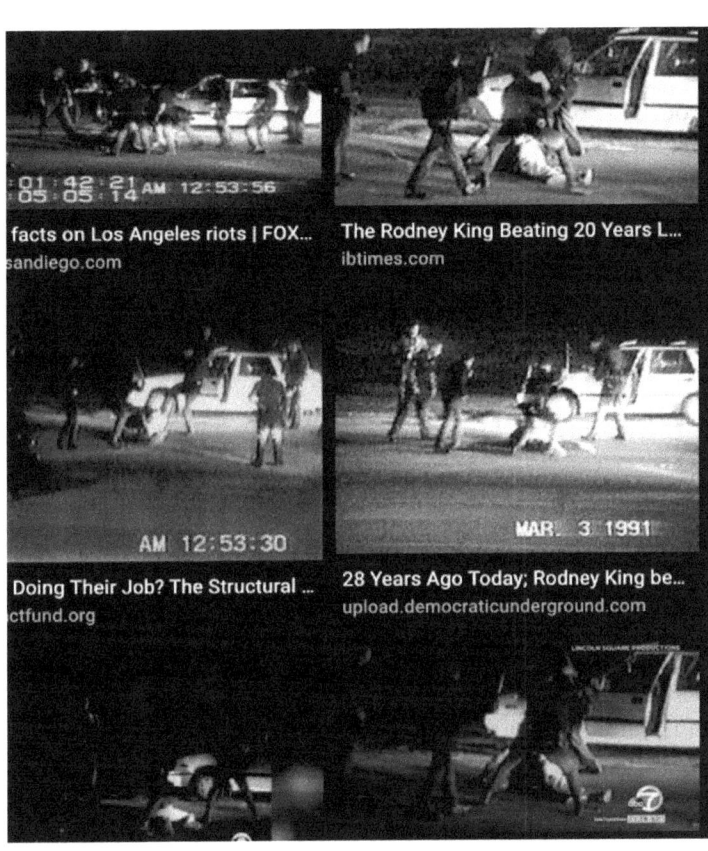

17 Work Footage (2020)

I have 462 songs in my iTunes library with the word love in the title.

A preoccupation, you might say. These songs do not include songs that are about love but don't mention *love at all*. They reside and operate in that space of longing and ellipses, like Luther Vandross' *if only for one night*, the title of which is a recurring refrain that he bequeaths continuously to an unknown disembodied interest in a beautiful and almost sorrowful compromise:

I won't tell a soul

No one has to know

If you want to be totally discreet

I'll be at your side

A roommate once told me: I know you've cooked as soon as I step through the door. *Don't your parents pay your rent?*

Asking just for a touch, even if it is accidental. A glance of acknowledgement only in the dark. A moment alone *just for one night*, one night, one night. An appeal in his voice backed by a chorus of women, standing at brightly silver microphones ready to support him, uttering *one night* as Vandross calms the desired. Easing their fears of exposure through the question of responsibility that consummation is laden with.

Eventually my flatmates exited the apartment to eat breakfast and to sleep again. The weekend is finite. I was left alone.

Vandross answers *no, I never have to hear from you again*. You can leave before the sun rises. I don't even need your name, I don't need to see you. *Let me hold you tight*, beating in your chest.

Trauma travels through bodies. In the blood, circling around the perimeter of the cell, liquid and quaking. The lash or sear or buckle under weight or volley is packaged and sent off across the terrain of time, lives, and apprehensions. We are born with that imprint dormant at our fingertips, staining the space between those crisscrossing lines on the skin of your hand.

A wave can move you. Beyond the push or pull. This is moving, as if to say: I feel the wave of that existence or persistence. You have transported me beyond my before. Being moved is about being stepped inside of.

Notice how the sun pierces the window with light. You feel the state of its heat. *What is that?* Human connection precedes the virtual network. Perhaps the virtual was always first embodied, the world a mess of entanglements shooting off and taking hold. *How did we ever think that we were?*

Bourgeois memory prolapse

The bright luminosity of New York can slide into blueblack darkness speckled with candle gold. Do you remember hiding away from light in the tucked corners of asphalt covered rooftops, warmed only by a blanket and a body that isn't yours?

We sought out light while splayed on rough grass, in a park field bounded by trees, camperdown elm, hornbeam. Friends fallen upon each other, shoes and socks cast aside so that feet can be cleansed with dry dirt. Dried apricots and sparkling water chase away any bubbling fear of a city of deliberate play, where one aspires to appear unbothered, unencumbered by a glaze of soft, intelligent eyes.

We tried to think of ideas to the furthest extent: what makes a city humane, the benefits of the occasional primal scream, how even the most conscientious of us still want power, why else would anyone live here.

That night we left the apartment with laughter, scrubbed and moisturized faces, mouthwash mint breath. We cooked separately but ate together. I chose an outfit purposefully banal, as to be noticeable. A collared shirt, of oxford, or flannel, or chambray, with a sweater pulled over it. Tonight, was cold. I learned the art of layering from my father, from whom I inherited not only a tall, lanky body, but also a disposition for middle class signifiers.

How we walked alongside each other, our muted joy, our brown and our white skin. We, as Baldwin might say, belonged to no where.

We could see inside the museum before we entered, the windows steamed from collective breath and body heat, a small afro puff wrapped in taut printed Dutch-Ghanaian fabric around the forehead of a guy from North Carolina who caught a bus to Brooklyn to labor for free, interning, just to leave, to get out and be here.

I stood in front of one piece, a tempest of lemon and mustard yellows, drunkenly musing to you, next to me, the short woman behind us, overhearing, admitted that she was the artist from Philadelphia, and somehow she appreciated my words about her vibrant matter.

On the fourth track of John Coltrane's *Meditations*, entitled 'Consequences,' the listener enters a musical space already commenced, the drum and piano placed beneath the surface and a saxophone that begins in a timbre, a color of sound, a burgundy or orange, that conveys a familiar musicality. A coherence descends, becomes gruff and sporadic, a biting of the reed perhaps, a stoppage of familiar notes as sound is caught in the throat of the horn, the reed now possibly bloodied, the horn held rough. The stress of the sound becomes heightened and the listening experience, for those not 'receptive' to the burgeoning screams, becomes more demanding, more physical, perhaps stress or frenzy producing, less 'pleasurable' in the way of harmony and softness.

How does one respond when fault lines have become the centers on which we rest? The world feels like it is constantly breaking. To say breaking, though, suggests the world was once whole.

I keep searching for unwhite territory, somewhere. Plush soft soil wet enough to stake a not flag of impossible escape. (what did you think was going to happen after we left?), that we could make a just world with energy bars and roaming impetus.

Out there in a valley that exists beyond thought. Concrete walls screen boundaries, and fluorescent light bulbs are the only materials that have ever been provided to you to make a home.

Later, sitting on firm caked earth under sun with small pockets of moisture that butterflies would drink from and scatter and surround me. I realized that I had brought no one with me to witness the allure.

And so, I dream of a person whispering close. How soft, how dependent the sound of the light, the trees that buckle ground above the tortoise visibly creeping without fear.

Mouth seismically to each other about every one, every thing we have lost. Speak just listen feel in this dream. We can admit it is more than fallen bodies in crevices between squares of sidewalk.

---

18 San Diego (2018)

The entire project of a country being founded on death. It's not how they don't cry with you as you place your hands to ears, a mother standing at sea, at the beach, arms flailing, screaming, thinking she has lost her child; it's to cry for family caught in a world of outside lawns and rounding corners, billboard over a lake flooding the sand bottom hiding in elaborate commons.

Force and lonesome are the possibilities of existing outside.

19 Costa Rica (2019)

CALIFORNIA

This morning, the blinds can't filter all the early gloss. Light swims through. I begin a series of goings. Shower. Warm, then reddening hot water. I dry off, eat, and walk a mile to the shore near my apartment in La Jolla.

A sidewalk, shivering from cars, leads to the park. At pauses, commissioned by traffic lights, I am the only movement, aside from an airbrushed shrub, the sun refracting on diamond glass from broken bottles tucked into the soil like glamourous landmines. I watch for onlookers, lay an emptied banana peel aside a tree root. I hope that it breaks down, feeds.

As a kid, I'd lift cinnamon-colored logs in my backyard, marveling at scurrying bug societies beneath, locking horns over how to redistribute the wealth of moisture and cellulose. I'd roll pill bugs between thumb and index without pressure so that I could blow the living sphere onto the field of lawn.

At the shore, I cradle my hands to pour the sea onto my face, tasting more than I should have of the aquatic brine. I press spongy plant buds, acting as a magnet for sand. I find myself always covered in sand. A dog, piqued by a crouching stranger, ventures over before being called away into existence by its owner.

I want to write a rhyming poem: sounds seas roundings Rikers. Cyclical cuffs. I want to be with someone in the way of gripping each shoulder bone so as not to fall. I don't want to like Europe like I once told P at the lake. But it's there and larger than constraint.

Drag a string on a bow. I listen for when strings bout. String theory meaning strung to a coupler socket. Dragged crisply in Jasper. Long as a number. Dying again, pulling everything. Tide drags my feet in its gravity. If you want to listen, the song is a Moon spilling blue light. Black boys gray as milk—a stringing soundtrack of our wakes.

On another morning, I hike early. The field—a curved flattened arrival—a hill—was a clearing. A stretch before I could see the sea. The dried grasses are tall bundles of blonde. Prickly and soft. I let my hands feather through as if the plants could ripple and bunch like smoke clouding the sky.

The dark billows seem near, grow denser. I once stood next to a white pick-up truck on fire. Turned sideways and emptied. At the shore, I draw a map in the sand of a country that won't exist. Imagine a dystopia where annual change is required. Every year every one would change homes, jobs, and locations in a revolving but never repetitious sequence. A world where one's position is never held.

Maybe I'm just thinking of how precarity is like falling. Maybe that world is just my life so far. As I write this Robert Mugabe has been in office for thirty-seven years.[20] I wish he and every other male in power would just leave. It's ok if that means I must leave, too.

---

20   Robert Mugabe is now dead

Where is the line around which one can walk around with the illusion of freedom? Where is the outside of here?

There's so much blood in my family. A grandma and an uncle bled out. Do you see the distancing there? Both my grandma and my uncle died violently. Is death ever not violent? Sometimes death is uneventful. I try to live a practice of love. No, I'm not sure what love *be*, in the most Komunyakaa way: 'I'm stone. (Lancôme) I'm flesh.'

Staying leaves nothing at stake, no urgency to mattering and becoming-together. Availability means why care. Three months in a city means each day is a day less in a finite well.

Leaving felt so arbitrary. A five-hour flight to sleep on an air mattress in California?

No one told me adulthood means sitting in rooms. I remember how we looked at each other, the way people who have seen each other naked do. I can barely find the language for this.

I told you that I hadn't met any Black people here (and felt so parochial for saying it). Not out of choice but because it wasn't an option. Staying rears power, but leaving is a release.

a certain coherence of its own terms

- intentioned/ disaggregated
- imperative
- materials-parallelism through
- disoriented
- narration/ narrative fragments
- experiences (affectivities)
- the structures of the page
- done, drone
- tuned up to the eye
- inside the interior world
- lyrical syntax break down
- appositionality

At an academic conference in Tennessee I stay at the same hostel as a professor from Delaware. Virginia Woolf once said: "How readily our thoughts swarm upon a new object". I ask if the professor was interested in putting hapticality into practice. A professor.

The professor walks me to my train to Atlanta the next morning. We shake hands. "Text me when you get there." Get where? I'm always going.

Stefano Harney says: "Hapticality occupies these rooms with a tap, tap…" Daft Punk references Emmanuel Levinas on *Face to Face*.

Claudia Rankine does, too.

I remember listening to her read in the basement of McNally Jackson. I couldn't see her face. Her voice said, "Then all life is a form of waiting, but it is the waiting of loneliness." Levinas says, "Memory replaces the past itself into this future." Maybe I'll spend my waiting looking for you in empty faces and open mouths.

There are questions here in California that float around. Pieces of angst charcoal. I followed the trajectory of a line of light being blocked by a fence. I was walking on Sunset Boulevard in every cliché. The light surrendered in the gaps between columns, becoming a strobe stammering down. Would such a moment of light constitute special effects or echo stagger? I can't decide if I am bored or if I am boring.

The buildings here in this cove of highways have little object presence. They funnel up onto the sky ambiguously holding bodies in stasis aside from the constant streams of cars. It is as if I slipped my hand under cold water.

Even amid the sprinklings of color I feel I've forgotten how to speak loudly. I can't claim exile but perhaps I can claim estrangement walking on the sides of roads. Students at my private school on the east coast organized a Black commencement. Critics said they should have gone to HBCUs if that is what they wanted.

Lips fuller than the entire campus.

River Bed

I walk daily through desiccated river beds. The electricity is off four hours each day. Some teachers and students would nap, cook, or play Civilization. I walk. For miles, in the winding valley, carrying water and a book.

The guards stop asking where I was going, simply waved me off from under the tree shade. I never gave them a clear answer because I only knew a few phrases in Somali. Sometimes the students would walk with me, wearing sandals. I looked down once, during a walk, and a student's foot was covered in blood. Shakir! We need to go get gauze.

He just smiled.

One day I became lost. I took a new route back to the school grounds. I ended up further out. Both sides of my eyes surrounded by orange brown clay that I could break off and crumble.

It rarely rained. There had been drought, and the gathering clouds were cause for joy even though it would be hours before I got back. I watched the sky darken. I listened to swinging bells hanging off the necks of goats and camels being called in, before the rain, by the farmers that always stared at me, the stranger sitting on the sand, alone.

21 Occupied Palestine (2018)

For:

My family (Sarakeo, Ashley, Baba Kenny, Tyrone, Isaac, Kia, and Ellen &&&)

Detroit.

Black people.

The cross-genre MFA program at UCSD: Camille Forbes, whose workshop this was started in, Brandon Som, ben doller, Sarah Hankins, Zachary, Alison, Ayden, Katherine, Noelle

Jordany and all the films

The writing communities at Cave Canem (Brooklyn), Callaloo, and the Watering Hole

Split/Lip Press

HIA friends (Aseem, esq.) , LREI, Abaarso and Somaliland, Ramallah, and Paris, I suppose . . .

& every writer that I have read or watched or listened to: this is all in response

About the Author

Calvin Walds is a writer, educator, and abolitionist/image-maker/nomad originally from Detroit, Michigan. His poems and texts have been published in *No, Dear*, *African-American Review*, *Hyperallergic*, *Callaloo Journal*, *the Poetry Project Newsletter*, *Ctrl-V Journal*, and are forthcoming in *DIAGRAM* and *Black Warrior Review*. As an educator, he has taught in Sunflower County, in the Mississippi Delta, Ramallah, in the Occupied Palestinean Territories, and most currently in New York City. He was a finalist for the Emerge Surface Be fellowship, the *Black Warrior Review* Poetry Contest, and long-listed for the *Cosmonauts Avenue* Poetry Prize. He comes from a transdisciplinary academic background, and is currently a MFA candidate at UCSD in Cross-Genre Writing. Right now, he is primarily interested in questions of fugitivity as an artistic practice and practice of resistance, anticolonial African cinema, the poetics of relation, assemblage, Black [always already] experimental music, and the painter Beauford Delaney's engagement with figuration and abstraction.

Flee is his first chapbook.

Now Available From

Split/Lip Press

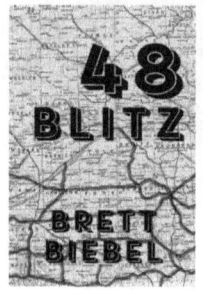

For more info about the press and our titles, visit

www.splitlippress.com

Follow us on Twitter and Instagram: @splitlippress

www.ingramcontent.com/pod-product-compliance
Lightning Source LLC
Chambersburg PA
CBHW060214050426
42446CB00013B/3070